C000146073

THIS BOOK BELONGS TO...

Name: Age:

Favourite player:

2018-2019

My Predictions...	Actual...
The Canaries' final position:	
The Canaries' top scorer:	
Championship winners:	
Championship top scorer:	
FA Cup winners:	
EFL Cup winners:	

Contributors: Dan Brigham & Peter Rogers

A TWOCAN PUBLICATION

©2018. Published by twocan under licence from Norwich City FC.

ISBN 978-1-912692-33-0

PICTURE CREDITS:
Action Images, Jasonpix, Press Association.

£9.95

CONTENTS

1 TIM KRUL

GOALKEEPER DOB: 03/04/1988 COUNTRY: NETHERLANDS

Tim joined the Canaries in the summer of 2018 from Newcastle United. He started his professional career with the Magpies in 2006, having previously been part of their youth academy and made 185 appearances before moving to Brighton in 2017. Krul has also represented the Netherlands at every level from U15 and was part of their team that came third at the 2014 FIFA World Cup.

2 IVO PINTO

DEFENDER DOB: 07/01/1990 COUNTRY: PORTUGAL

Norwich City signed Ivo from Dinamo Zagreb in January 2016, where the full-back made over 100 appearances over two seasons, helping the Blues to consecutive Croatian titles as well as Croatian Cup and Super Cup successes.

SQUAD 2018-19

4 BEN GODFREY

MIDFIELDER   **DOB: 15/01/1998**   **COUNTRY: ENGLAND**

After signing from York City in January 2016 on his 18th birthday, Ben came off the bench for his senior Canaries debut in an EFL Cup second round tie with Coventry City in August 2016 and scored the final goal in a 6-1 victory.

6 CHRISTOPH ZIMMERMANN

DEFENDER   **DOB: 12/01/1993**   **COUNTRY: GERMANY**

Christoph joined the Canaries on a free transfer in July 2017, following Head Coach Daniel Farke from Borussia Dortmund II. The German centre-half skippered the side during Farke's leadership at Dortmund II.

7 BEN MARSHALL

MIDFIELDER   **DOB: 29/03/1991**   **COUNTRY: ENGLAND**

Ben, who began his career at Manchester United at the age of seven, arrived at Carrow Road in the summer from newly-promoted Wolves. He has also been capped for England U21s, making his debut in a 2-0 victory over Azerbaijan in 2012.

8 MARIO VRANČIĆ

MIDFIELDER   **DOB: 23/05/1989**   **COUNTRY: BOSNIA & HERZEGOVINA**

Mario was born in the city of Slavonski Brod in what was formerly known as Yugoslavia, but moved to Germany with his family at the age of five. After playing for his adopted nation at a number of youth levels, he was given the go-ahead by FIFA to represent his homeland's senior side.

9 NÉLSON OLIVEIRA

FORWARD   **DOB: 08/08/1991**   **COUNTRY: PORTUGAL**

Nelson joined the Canaries from Portuguese side Benfica in August 2016, but while with the Lisbon club, he hit the back of the net on his Champions League debut Zenit St Petersburg in 2012. Big and strong, the Portugal international played three games at Euro 2012 as his country reached the semi-finals before being beaten by eventual champions Spain.

10 MORITZ LEITNER

MIDFIELDER   **DOB: 08/12/1992**   **COUNTRY: GERMANY**

During the summer of 2018, Moritz made his City loan deal a permanent one, signing a four-year contact with the Canaries. His first City goal secured a point at Portman Road in September and stretched the Canaries' unbeaten run against arch-rivals Ipswich Town to 11 games.

11 JORDAN **RHODES**

FORWARD   **DOB: 05/02/1990**   **COUNTRY: SCOTLAND**

Scottish international striker Jordan is on a season-long loan from Championship rivals Sheffield Wednesday. Approaching 400 league appearances, the hard-working striker has scored over 180 goals in his career and while at Huddersfield Town in 2011-12, he was the top scorer in England with 36 league goals.

12 JAMAL LEWIS

DEFENDER   **DOB: 25/01/1998**   **COUNTRY: NORTHERN IRELAND**

Before choosing to play football for Norwich City, Jamal was a national champion athlete competing over 1500m and 800m. Although he was born in England, Lewis is eligible, through his mother, to play for Northern Ireland and earned his first cap in a 2-1 friendly win over South Korea in March 2018.

16 MATT JARVIS

MIDFIELDER   **DOB: 22/05/1986**   **COUNTRY: ENGLAND**

Matt began his senior career at Gillingham, moving to Wolverhampton Wanderers and then West Ham United before settling at Carrow Road. He also has one England cap to his name, coming on as a substitute during a 1-1 draw with Ghana at Wembley Stadium in 2011.

15 TIMM KLOSE

DEFENDER   **DOB: 09/05/1988**   **COUNTRY: SWITZERLAND**

Timm signed for City in January 2016 from German club Wolfsburg, where his impressive displays helped the Wolves win the German Cup and German Super Cup. After a successful start to his Norwich career, Klose scored his first goal for the Canaries in a vital 3–2 win over Newcastle United at Carrow Road in April 2016.

17 EMILIANO BUENDÍA

MIDFIELDER   **DOB: 25/12/1996**   **COUNTRY: ARGENTINA**

Born in Argentina, Emiliano was at Real Madrid as a youngster and made the move to Carrow Road in the summer of 2018 from Spanish Club Getafe. The attacking midfielder, who is an exciting prospect, can also perform on the wing.

18 MARCO STIEPERMANN

MIDFIELDER   **DOB: 09/02/1991**   **COUNTRY: GERMANY**

The versatile German midfielder, who began his career at Borussia Dortmund, joined the club at the start of the 2017-18 season from German outfit VfL Bochum. Marco has represented his home nation at every level from U15 to U20.

19 TOM TRYBULL

MIDFIELDER   **DOB: 09/03/1993**   **COUNTRY: GERMANY**

Tom joined City in August 2017 from Dutch side ADO Den Haag. Although a defence-minded midfielder, he scored his first goal for the club on his debut, in the EFL Cup 4–1 home win over Charlton Athletic and netted his first league goal for the Canaries in a 2-1 home win over Millwall in January 2018.

23 KENNY McLEAN

MIDFIELDER **DOB: 08/01/1992** **COUNTRY: SCOTLAND**

Scottish International Kenny joined Norwich City from Aberdeen in January 2018, but was loaned back to the Dons until the end of the 2017-18 campaign. In his first game for the Canaries, he opened the scoring with a superb free-kick in a 3-1 pre-season win at League Two Lincoln City.

22 TEEMU PUKKI

FORWARD **DOB: 29/03/1990** **COUNTRY: FINLAND**

A Finland international with over 60 caps to his name, Teemu join the club in the summer of 2018 from Brøndby in Denmark and began his City Career in fine form, netting his first goal in front of the Norwich fans against WBA.

24 FELIX PASSLACK

DEFENDER **DOB: 29/05/1998** **COUNTRY: GERMANY**

City signed the German youth international defender Felix Passlack on a season-long loan from Bundesliga side Borussia Dortmund. Felix reunited at Carrow Road with Canaries boss Daniel Farke, who previously coached the 20-year-old at Dortmund.

27 ALEXANDER TETTEY

MIDFIELDER   **DOB: 04/04/1986**   **COUNTRY: NORWAY**

Alex was born in the Ghanaian capital of Accra, but moved to Norway as a youngster, and spent six seasons at Rosenborg from 2003-09. While there, he won the Norwegian title and played 12 games in the Champions League - including a European debut away to Real Madrid. He moved to Carrow Road from French side Rennes in August 2012.

25 ONEL HERNÁNDEZ

MIDFIELDER   **DOB: 01/02/1993**   **COUNTRY: GERMANY**

Onel arrived at Carrow Road in January 2018 from Eintracht Braunschweig. The Cuban-born German winger started the season in blistering form, scoring twice in the opening day fixture at Birmingham City, including a dramatic late equaliser to take a point away from St Andrew's.

30 CARLTON MORRIS

FORWARD   **DOB: 16/12/1995**   **COUNTRY: ENGLAND**

Carlton began his career at Norwich City at the age of 11. He spent the 2017-18 season on loan to Shrewsbury Town, making two trips to Wembley, once in the Checkatrade Trophy final after scoring in the semi-final win over Yeovil and again for the League One Play-Off final after scoring against Charlton in the second leg of the Play-Off semi-final.

31 GRANT **HANLEY**

DEFENDER   DOB: **20/11/1991**   COUNTRY: **SCOTLAND**

The Scottish international is a player who leads by example and since signing from Newcastle United at the beginning of last season, club captain Grant has become a commanding presence in the City backline.

33 MICHAEL **McGOVERN**

GOALKEEPER   DOB: **12/07/1984**   COUNTRY: **NORTHERN IRELAND**

Before joining the Canaries in 2016, Michael enjoyed success in Scotland, winning the Scottish Challenge Cup with Ross County and Falkirk, keeping clean sheets in both finals. He is a regular for his national team and starred in Northern Ireland's Euro 2016 campaign.

32 DENNIS **SRBENY**

FORWARD   DOB: **05/05/1994**   COUNTRY: **GERMANY**

Dennis arrived at the club during the January 2018 transfer window from German side SC Paderborn. His first taste of Carrow Road came in the East Anglian derby, when Timm Klose's 90th minute header rescued the most dramatic of points and he scored his first league goal in April 2018 in a 3-1 home win against Villa.

34 LOUIS **THOMPSON**

MIDFIELDER   DOB: **19/12/1994**   COUNTRY: **WALES**

Louis signed for City from Swindon Town on transfer deadline day in September 2014. His Canaries debut came in the 6-1 EFL Cup win over Coventry City in August 2016 and he made five further appearances before suffering a long-term Achilles injury that ruled him out for the remainder of the season. He enjoyed a great pre-season and is battling his way back to full fitness.

36 TODD CANTWELL

MIDFIELDER   DOB: 27/02/1998   COUNTRY: ENGLAND

Todd joined the Norwich Academy at the age of 10. He made his senior debut in January 2018 in an FA Cup match against Chelsea at Stamford Bridge, before being loaned to Fortuna Sittard for the second half of the 2017-18 season. At the start of this term, Cantwell made his first start for City in the first round EFL Cup 3-1 victory over Stevenage.

37 MAX AARONS

DEFENDER   DOB: 04/01/2000   COUNTRY: ENGLAND

Max has been with the Club since 2016 after joining from Luton Town and following an impressive season with City's development squads, the youngster made his senior debut this season in the EFL cup against Stevenage. He added a goal in the 3-1 second round win at Cardiff City and made an impressive Championship debut against Ipswich Town at Portman Road in September.

38 ASTON OXBOROUGH

GOALKEEPER   DOB: 09/05/1998   COUNTRY: ENGLAND

Local lad and City fan, Aston joined the club's Academy system at the age of 10 playing as a defender, but soon moved back and put on the goalkeeper's gloves. Now standing 6' 5", Oxborough looks to have a great future between the sticks.

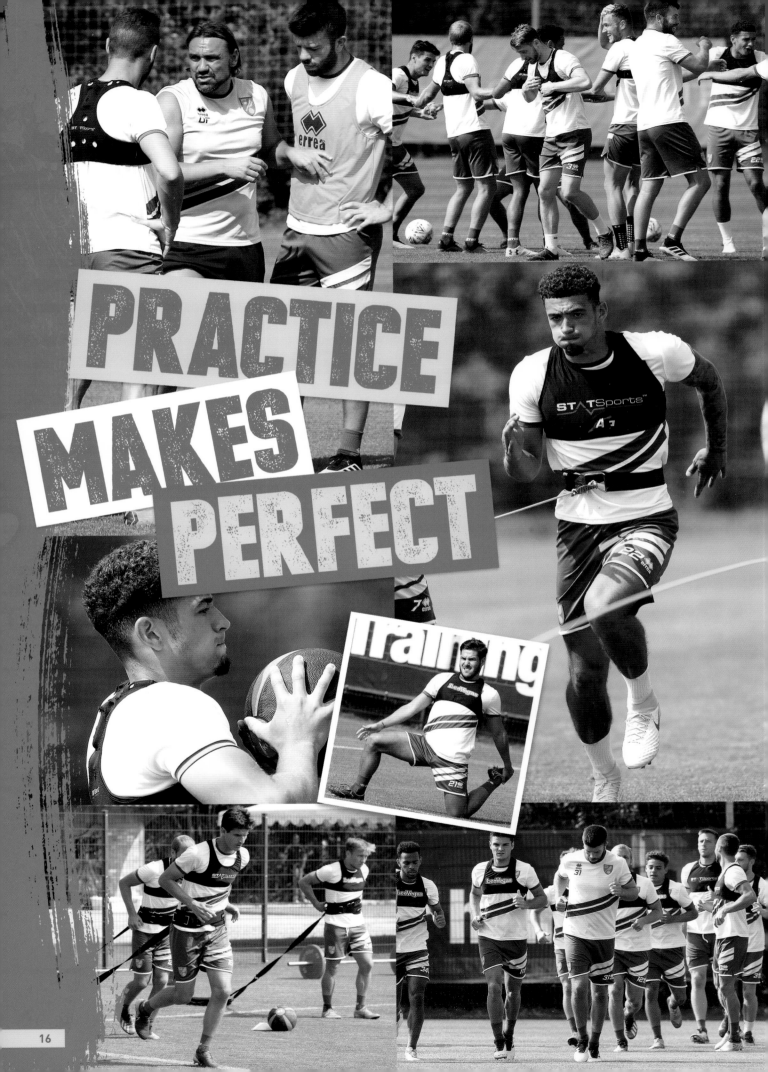

PRACTICE MAKES PERFECT

Practice, preparation and perseverance are all well-known key ingredients to success in the modern game. Long before the Canaries run out at Carrow Road, they will have gone through a thorough and detailed spell of work at the club's busy training centre.

The Canaries' training ground is geared up to ensure that Daniel Farke's men are fully equipped for the Championship challenges that lie ahead. The modern-day player will not only be given the best of surfaces to practice on, but also given the very best advice and guidance in terms of their fitness, diet, rest and mental approach to performing at their maximum.

A typical day will begin with a series of physical tests, being weighed and taking part in a number of aerobic exercises, before blood levels and heart rates are measured.

Diet is vital to any player's wellbeing and performance levels, so a suitable breakfast is provided before the players head to the gym to enjoy their own personal work-outs.

Prior to taking to the training pitches, players will be provided with a GPS tracking system and heart rate analysis monitors ensuring that all they do can be measured, monitored and reviewed. Then the physical conditioning begins out on the pitches. The manager and coaches will get down to working on various drills, set-piece situations and practice matches in the day's main session.

After a warm-down programme, it's off for a healthy lunch and a return to the gym for a strength, power and injury presentation session and feedback on the day's activities will be provided to the manager, coaches and players by the sports science department.

Come match day, this is where all the team's hard work and dedication through the week will make the difference.

MORITZ
LEITNER

Magic MOMENT

87'

BARHAM **7**

BURLEY **2**
DONOWA **11**
CHANNON **8**

6 BUTCHER
12 SUNDERLAND

1 COOPER
7 PUTTNEY

ZONDERVAN **4**
DEEHAN **9** CRANSON
5 **4** BRUCE
10 DOZZELL
3 McCALL

WATSON **6**

4 BRUCE

GATES **11**
HARFORD **10**

WE'RE GOING TO *Wembley*

FIXTURE: Milk Cup semi-final second leg

DATE: Wednesday, March 6, 1985

SCORE: Norwich City 2 Ipswich Town 0

VENUE: Carrow Road

ATTENDANCE: 23,545

Steve Bruce etched his name into Norwich City folklore when his bullet header three minutes from time sealed the Canaries' dramatic Milk Cup semi-final victory over arch-rivals Ipswich Town in 1985.

After the first leg of this semi-final had ended 1-0 to Ipswich, Norwich levelled the tie on aggregate thanks to John Deehan's first-half strike.

The match looked to be heading for extra time until Bruce met a Mark Barham corner and planted a powerful header past Paul Cooper to send City to Wembley.

After being the hero of the hour in the semi-final, Bruce was then voted Man of the Match in the 1-0 victory over Sunderland in the final.

Watch out for these Danger Men
when the Canaries meet their
Championship rivals...

DANGER MEN

ASTON VILLA

Jack Grealish

Attacking midfielder Jack Grealish is sure to be the driving force behind Aston Villa once again in 2018/19.

The talented playmaker is a Villa fan and will be going full throttle to help Steve Bruce's side win promotion back to the Premier League. Villa were delighted to keep him at the club following a summer of speculation about the England under-21 star's future.

BOLTON WANDERERS

Will Buckley

Attacking midfielder Will Buckley joined Bolton Wanderers in the summer of 2017 and adds a great deal of experience to the Bolton ranks.

He made 26 appearances for Phil Parkinson's side last season as Wanderers successfully maintained their Championship status. His fine form has continued into the new 2018-19 campaign with the former Brighton man netting his first goal of the season in a 2-2 draw at home to Bristol City in August.

BIRMINGHAM CITY

Che Adams

After joining Blues from Sheffield United in August 2016, all-action midfielder Che Adams wasted little time in showing the St Andrew's faithful just what he was all about.

Adams wrote his name into Birmingham City folklore on the final day of the 2016-17 campaign, scoring the goal that preserved the club's Championship status. He is sure to be a key player for Garry Monk's men in 2018-19.

BRENTFORD

Ollie Watkins

One of the most exciting and talented footballers outside of the Premier League, Ollie Watkins has been a roaring success since joining Brentford from Exeter City in the summer of 2017.

He netted an impressive eleven goals in all competitions in his first season at Griffin Park. He loves to let fly from distance and has scored a number of spectacular goals for the Bees.

BLACKBURN ROVERS

Elliott Bennett

Experienced winger Elliott Bennett played a vital role in Rovers' promotion from League One in 2017-18.

The former Norwich man has been a great influence on the younger players at Ewood Park and will be an important member of Tony Mowbray's team once again now they are back in the Championship.

BRISTOL CITY

Andreas Weimann

Much-travelled Austrian striker Andreas Weimann joined Bristol City ahead of the 2018-19 season, agreeing a three-year deal at Ashton Gate.

Weimann is a vastly experienced forward who knows the English game well following spells with Aston Villa, Watford, Derby County and Wolves. The Robins will be looking for Weimann to grab the goals to fire them into Play-Off contention.

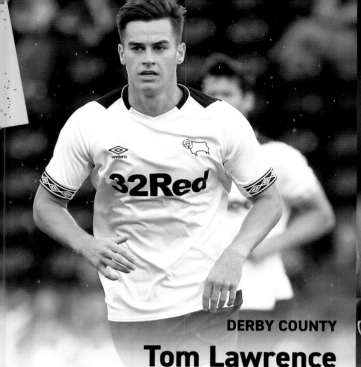

DERBY COUNTY
Tom Lawrence

Wales international midfielder Tom Lawrence looks set to play a vital role at Pride Park in 2018-19 under new Derby boss Frank Lampard.

The Rams' midfielder certainly has an eye for goal and with Lampard to guide him, Lawrence could well become one of the Championship's star turns over the coming months. He began the season in fine form with two goals in Derby's opening two games.

LEEDS UNITED
Patrick Bamford

A proven goalscorer in the Championship, Patrick Bamford joined Leeds United in the summer of 2018 from Middlesbrough.

Bamford is a great finisher, who also has great awareness of those around him. His arrival at Elland Road has certainly heightened the levels of expectation among the Leeds United fans.

HULL CITY
Fraizer Campbell

Vastly-experienced striker Fraizer Campbell brings an enormous amount of knowhow to the Tigers' front line.

A former England international, Campbell has spent time on the books at some of the country's biggest clubs including Manchester United and Tottenham Hotspur. Now in his second spell with Hull, he was on target against Sheffield Wednesday to ensure the Tigers' first point of the 2018-19 season.

MIDDLESBROUGH
Britt Assombalonga

Former Nottingham Forest striker Britt Assombalonga joined Middlesbrough in July 2015 for a club record fee of £15M.

He was a consistent goalscorer with both Peterborough United and Forest. Assombalonga netted 13 goals as Boro reached the Play-Off semi-finals last season. Boro will be looking for him to be heavily among the goals again in 2018-19 as they look to mount a successful promotion bid.

IPSWICH TOWN
Jon Nolan

Talented midfielder Jon Nolan was an instrumental player for Shrewsbury Town in 2017-18 as the Shrews reached both the Checkatrade Trophy final and the League One Play-Off final.

In August 2018, he joined Ipswich Town and reunited with his former Shrewsbury boss Paul Hurst who took over at Portman Road three months earlier. Nolan is expected to flourish at Championship level.

MILLWALL
Steve Morison

Former City forward Steve Morison is currently enjoying his second spell with the Lions.

His goals helped propel the South London club to the verge of the Play-Offs last season. Approaching 300 games for Millwall and almost 100 goals, Morison is a vital member of Neil Harris' squad with a positive influence both on and off the pitch.

Watch out for these Danger Men when the Canaries meet their Championship rivals...

DANGER MEN

QUEENS PARK RANGERS

Eberechi Eze

After spending a loan spell with Wycombe Wanderers last season, Eze has returned to Loftus Road and cemented himself a place in the heart of the Hoops' midfield.

A true box-to-box midfielder, Eze loves to plough forward and lend his support to attacking situations. The 20-year-old produced a number of eye-catching displays at the start of the 2018/19 season and was on target in Rangers' first home game of the campaign against Sheffield United.

NOTTINGHAM FOREST

Lewis Grabban

A proven Championship goalscorer, Lewis Grabban joined Nottingham Forest in July 2018 for a fee believed to have been in the region of £6M.

His arrival at the City Ground is expected to relieve some of the pressure for goals on fellow frontman Daryl Murphy. Former Canary Grabban has played for a host of clubs and appears to have the handy knack of always taking his scoring boots with him.

READING

Jon Dadi Bodvarsson

Icelandic international forward Jon Dadi Bodvarsson has become something of a cult hero with Reading fans at the Madejski Stadium after netting ten goals for the Royals last season.

He represented his country at the 2018 World Cup finals in Russia and also netted Reading's first goal of the new 2018-19 campaign.

PRESTON NORTH END

Tom Barkhuizen

After beginning his career with Preston's rivals Blackpool, striker Tom Barkhuizen is a player who will be looking to make his mark for Alex Neil's side in 2018-19.

A string of loan spells with Hereford United, Fleetwood Town and Morecambe resulted in a permanent switch to Morecambe and it was his goalscoring form at the Globe Arena that alerted North End who signed him in November 2016.

ROTHERHAM UNITED

Joe Newell

Versatile midfielder Joe Newell was one of the Millers' heroes as Rotherham United won promotion to the Championship via the League One Play-Offs.

With the ability to operate in a creative central midfield berth or out on the wing, Newell was almost ever-present for the Millers last season and will be a key performer for Paul Warne's men in their 2018-19 Championship campaign.

SHEFFIELD UNITED
Billy Sharp

Now in his third spell with the Blades, and still looking as lively as ever in front of goal, Billy Sharp will once again be at the forefront of manager Chris Wilder's thoughts at Bramall Lane

Sharp became the Sheffield United captain in 2016 and is now closing in on 200 goals for the club.

SWANSEA CITY
Oliver McBurnie

Following a highly productive loan spell in the Championship with Barnsley in the second-half of last season, Oliver McBurnie has earned the chance to lead the line for Swansea City as the Welsh club bid to bounce back to the top-flight in 2018-19.

McBurnie scored nine goals in 17 outings for a struggling Tykes team last season and will now look to grab his Swansea opportunity with both hands.

SHEFFIELD WEDNESDAY
Fernando Forestieri

The jewel in Sheffield Wednesday's crown, all eyes at Hillsborough will once again be on skilful Italian Fernando Forestieri who is the man that makes the Owls tick.

The Wednesday fans will be looking for Forestieri to inspire those around him as the club searches for an improved season under Jos Luhakay.

WEST BROMWICH ALBION
Jay Rodriguez

Burnley-born England striker Jay Rodriguez began his career at his hometown club before moving on to the Premier League with Southampton and then West Bromwich Albion.

A cool customer with the ball at his feet, Rodriguez has all the skills to really shine in the Championship for an Albion side who will hope their stay in the second-tier is a brief one.

STOKE CITY
Benik Afobe

Striker Benik Afobe is the man charged with scoring the goals to fire Stoke City back to the Premier League at the first time of asking.

Afobe joined the Potters on loan from Wolverhampton Wanderers in June 2018 and his physical presence and goal threat are sure to play a huge part in the Potters' 2018-19 promotion push.

WIGAN ATHLETIC
Nick Powell

Midfielder Nick Powell was nominated for the EFL League One Player of the Season award after an outstanding season in the Latics' 2017-18 title-winning campaign.

A technically gifted player with the ability to score goals and create chances for others, Powell will certainly be one of the first names on Paul Cook's teamsheet as Wigan look to establish themselves at Championship level.

BORN:

IWAN WYN ROBERTS
JUNE 26, 1968 · BANGOR, WALES

POSITION:

STRIKER

CANARIES DEBUT:

NORWICH CITY 0-2 WOLVES
NATIONWIDE DIVISION ONE
AUGUST 9, 1997

CITY PLAYER OF THE SEASON:

1998-99 & 1999-2000

Striker Iwan Roberts scored an impressive 96 goals for the Canaries between 1997 and 2004. Roberts was signed by Mike Walker from Wolves for a fee of £850,000 in the summer of 1997.

Despite a disappointing first season in Norfolk, Roberts went on to become one of the Carrow Road crowd's all-time favourite players.

He was twice voted player of the season and won a place in the inaugural Hall of Fame during the Centenary celebrations. Roberts captained City in their 2001-02 Play-Off final against Birmingham in the Millennium Stadium and also chipped in with vital goals during the 2003-04 Nationwide First Division title-winning campaign.

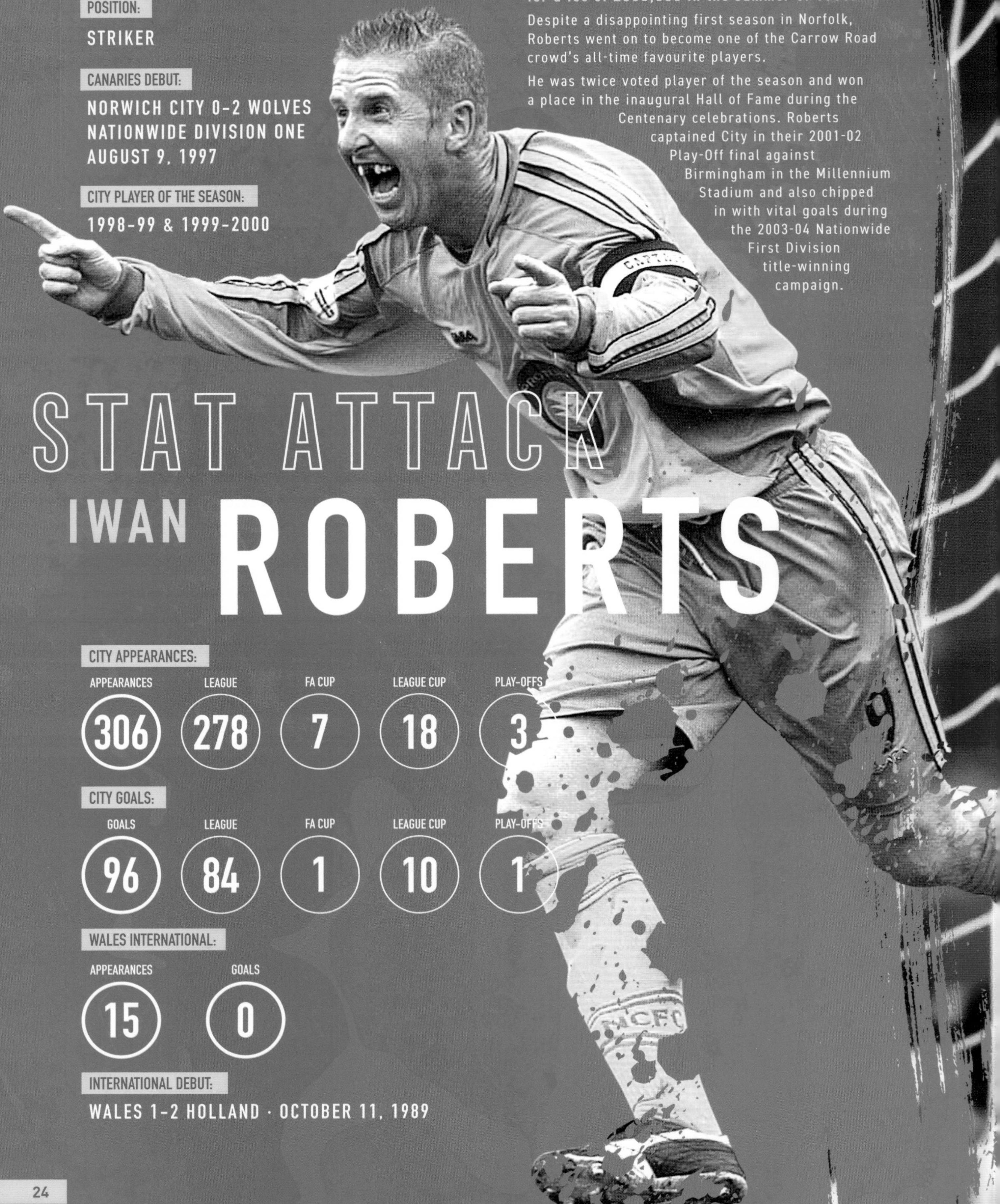

STAT ATTACK
IWAN ROBERTS

CITY APPEARANCES:

APPEARANCES	LEAGUE	FA CUP	LEAGUE CUP	PLAY-OFFS
306	278	7	18	3

CITY GOALS:

GOALS	LEAGUE	FA CUP	LEAGUE CUP	PLAY-OFFS
96	84	1	10	1

WALES INTERNATIONAL:

APPEARANCES	GOALS
15	0

INTERNATIONAL DEBUT:

WALES 1-2 HOLLAND · OCTOBER 11, 1989

TIM KRUL

FAN'TASTIC

There are five England World Cup stars hiding in the crowd... Can you spot them?

ANSWERS ON PAGE 62

Ferenc Puskas is one of the greatest footballers of all time and the creator of the famous 'V' move that you can see used in most games of football.

It allows you to change direction quickly and fool your defender. The move is very simple, but hard to master at speed.

THE PUSKAS MOVE
#BOY'SGOTSKILLS

TIP:
Use this move when you need to lose your defender. Pretend to strike the ball, your opponent will move to block your faked shot, allowing you to move freely in another direction.

TIP:
Always wait until your defender lunges for the ball before performing the Puskas move.

1. Start by dribbling the ball, keep it as near to your foot as possible while moving forward.

2. Move as if to kick the ball, but rather than striking it, bring your foot over the top of the ball.

TIP:
Don't perform this move too often or your opponents will learn to expect it!

3. Use the bottom of your foot to quickly drag the ball back to you.

4. Now change direction. You can finish the move with a shot at goal or by passing to a teammate.

TEEMU PUKKI

22

Have fun colouring this picture of Teemu Pukki...

JORDAN RHODES

Magic MOMENT

51'

Norwich City became the only British team to defeat Bayern Munich in the Olympic Stadium, when they recorded a 2-1 triumph over the German giants in their 1993-94 UEFA Cup meeting.

Goals from Jeremy Goss and Mark Bowen ensured Norwich pulled off that memorable second round, first leg triumph in Munich. City then faced the challenge of completing the job when the two sides met for the second leg at Carrow Road.

The visitors took an early lead before the Canaries' Euro hero Jeremy Goss stuck once again. Goss' second-half equaliser at the Barclay End ensured match ended 1-1 and City won the tie 3-2 on aggregate.

1 AUMANN

HELMER 5

MATTHAUS 10

9 SUTTON

11 GOSS

ZIEGE 3

7 EADIE

SCHUPP 8

KREUZER 4

JORGINHO 2

FOX 10

3 BOWEN

WOUTERS 7

8 CROOK

EUROPEAN *Glory*

FIXTURE: UEFA Cup second round second leg

DATE: Wednesday, November 3, 1993

SCORE: Norwich City 1 Bayern Munich 1

VENUE: Carrow Road

ATTENDANCE: 20,829

PLAYER OF THE SEASON

JAMES MADDISON

Stats often only tell half a story. James Maddison's 14 goals - the most by anyone in a yellow and green shirt last season - and eight assists are numerical proof that a player has had a fantastic season. But anyone who saw Maddison will know he contributed far more than just goals and assists, as important as they were.

From an early age, special things were expected of Maddison. Two footed, dexterous, quick-witted, confident and with an eye for a killer goal or pass, Maddison came good on his promise last season. And then some.

The way he riled the opposition fans was testament to his great ability. He was a constant threat - whether swerving his way past challenges, scoring from 25 yards or causing havoc with his movement - and the fans, players and managers of opposing teams knew it. Often, they could do very little about it.

Maddison had made only three appearances for City the previous season - he did, of course, score on his Championship debut - and while a loan move to Aberdeen went well, there was a danger that such a talent might have started to drift.

But Stuart Webber offered him a new contract in pre-season, and Daniel Farke trusted Maddison to the extent that he went from hoping to be part of the squad at the start of the season to becoming the main man from kick-off.

Winning goals at Middlesbrough, Ipswich, Bristol City, Brentford and at home to Millwall and Reading - many of them spectacular strikes - guaranteed that in a season of ups and downs for Norwich, Maddison was constantly providing fireworks.

It was no surprise that he won the Barry Butler Memorial Trophy at the end of the season, and no surprise that he became Norwich City's biggest ever transfer out when he got a Premier League move to Leicester City. He belongs on the biggest stage, and it was a privilege to see such an enormous talent in a yellow and green shirt.

JOSH MURPHY

NORWICH 3-1 ASTON VILLA
APRIL 7, 2018

Josh Murphy had no right to score from there. It was too far out, too unlikely. The match, played in front of the Sky TV cameras, was meandering to half-time with the score stuck at 0-0. Little that had gone before hinted at the magic that was about to happen.

Murphy, on the right, picks up the ball from a James Maddison pass. When he receives it, he's 10 yards out from the right-hand corner of the penalty box. He takes two touches with his right foot to amble more centrally, and finds himself 30 yards out, on his left foot, side-on to the goal. A Villa player, sensing the danger, rushes out to block him, but he's far, far too late.

With little backlift, Murphy strikes the ball sweetly. It has far to travel, but Murphy has found the perfect trajectory, looping the ball powerfully down and up and into the top far corner. Sam Johnstone, in the Villa goal, has time to react due to the distance from which it was hit, but no one under 7ft tall was getting anywhere near to it.
The net bulges, Carrow Road erupts.

The flight, the distance, the curve all added up to make it a thing of beauty.

It was also testament to Murphy's belief in his own long-range shooting, for he had missed a couple of efforts already. But that didn't get him down; instead, perhaps, it spurred him on to even greater heights. In a season of sensational goals, it was Murphy's strike that deservedly won the fans' Goal of the Season award.

GOAL
OF THE SEASON

GUESS THE CLUB

Can you
work out which
European Club
each set of clues is pointing to?

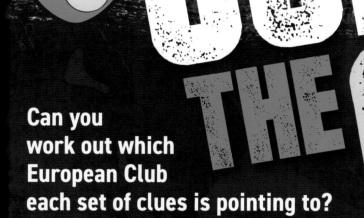

1 ANSWER

3 ANSWER

2 ANSWER

4 ANSWER

5 ANSWER

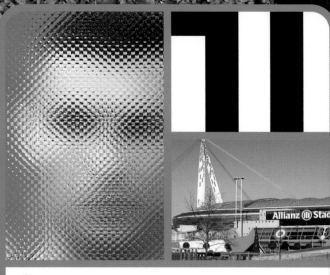

8 ANSWER

6 ANSWER

9 ANSWER

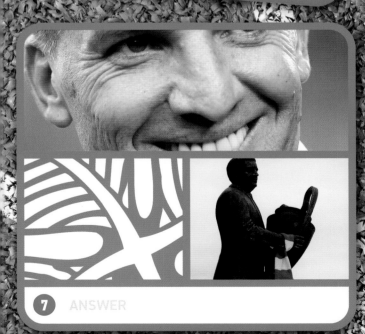

7 ANSWER

10 ANSWER

ANSWERS ON PAGE 62

LOCAL HEROES

The Pride of Anglia. You'll hear - and probably use - that phrase in the build-up to any East Anglian derby. You'll also hear it during the game, after the game and on social media constantly. To Norwich and Ipswich fans, little matters more than winning the derby, and claiming their team to be the Pride of Anglia.

The sides first faced each other professionally in 1939 - we won't mention the score – and have met a further 105 times.

As club fortunes have swung, so have East Anglian derby fortunes. Norwich City have dominated recently, with a whole host of new heroes emerging. No Norwich fan will ever forget the 2010-11 season, when Paul Lambert's men tore Ipswich apart 4-1 and 5-1 on their way to a second successive promotion; there was very doubt where the Pride of Anglia laid that season.

Sometimes, it's not even the wins that always live longest in the memory. After all, who will forget Timm Klose rising above the Ipswich defence in the 95th minute to equalise for City just six minutes after Ipswich had taken the lead? The roar from the Norwich fans, silencing the celebrating Town supporters, was one of the great moments in East Anglian derby history.

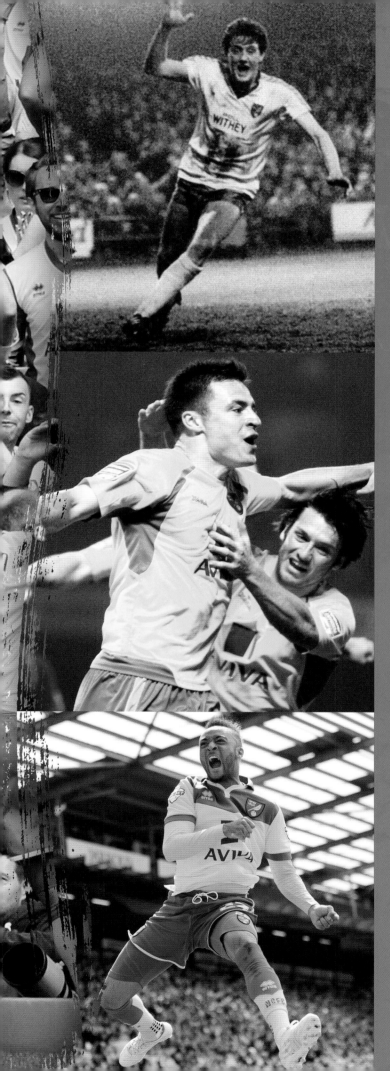

NORWICH 2-0 IPSWICH

MILK CUP SEMI-FINAL, SECOND LEG, MARCH 1985

It was the latest of late shows, and it was settled by what may be the most famous goal in East Anglian derby history.

Ipswich had taken a 1-0 lead into the second leg of the Milk Cup semi-final, but John Deehan's deflected strike in the 35th minute at Carrow Road levelled the tie. As nerves started to shred, the second half became a series of wild tackles and skirmishes.

Chances were few and far between and, as the tie looked destined for extra time, City forced a corner on the left in the 87th minute. Mark Barham rushed over to take it, and swung in a far post corner that Steve Bruce thundered powerfully into the top corner. The noise was deafening as Bruce and his teammates wheeled away in manic celebration. The final whistle brought more jubilation, with City on their way to Wembley.

IPSWICH 1-5 NORWICH

CHAMPIONSHIP, APRIL 2011

A Grant Holt hat-trick had already put Ipswich to the sword at Carrow Road in November in a 4-1 win. Now, six months later, there was even more at stake as Norwich headed down the A140 to Portman Road: promotion to the Premier League. A win would take City back into the top two, while a win for Ipswich would have moved them just three points off the Play-Offs.

From Andrew Surman's opening goal on 13 minutes, the result was never in doubt. Norwich ripped apart Ipswich, and the match report in the Daily Telegraph summed up the night: "These are the nights that Norwich City fans dream of, watching their terrific team tear apart their biggest rivals away from home. Move after move, goal after goal, chant after chant. This wasn't Old Farm; this was slaughterhouse."

An own goal from Gareth McAuley, and strikes from Simeon Jackson, Danny Pacheco and Russell Martin completed the rout, with the Norwich fans singing "Are you watching Carrow Road" to the 7,000 watching the game on a beamback. What a night.

NORWICH 3-1 IPSWICH

CHAMPIONSHIP PLAY-OFF SEMI-FINAL, SECOND LEG, MAY 2015

Perhaps the biggest game in East Anglian derby history. The Milk Cup semi-final runs it close, of course, but with a play-off final place at stake - and all of those Premier League riches - 90 minutes of Norwich v Ipswich action has never meant more.

The first leg at Portman Road had finished 1-1, with Paul Anderson's strike cancelling out Jonny Howson's, setting up the second leg at Carrow Road nicely. City, who had finished third in the Championship after a brilliant run under new manager Alex Neil, were the favourites - and had to deal with all of the pressure that came with it.

After a nervy, stodgy first half, the game went into overdrive after half-time. Norwich came out all-guns blazing and Christophe Berra was sent off in the 50th minute for handling Nathan Redmond's goal-bound effort. Wes Hoolahan stepped up to take the penalty and found the corner to give Norwich a deserved lead. But 10 minutes later Tommy Smith scrambled in a goal from a free-kick to level the scores, but that just made City play even better. A fine finish from Nathan Redmond gave City the lead on 64 minutes and Cameron Jerome made the game safe 12 minutes later. Cue a pitch invasion at full-time, and another trip to Wembley.

BORN:

BRYAN JAMES GUNN
DECEMBER 22, 1963 · THURSO, SCOTLAND

POSITION:

GOALKEEPER

CANARIES DEBUT:

NORWICH CITY 2-1 COVENTRY CITY
FULL MEMBERS CUP
NOVEMBER 4, 1986

CITY PLAYER OF THE SEASON:

1987-88 & 1992-93

STAT ATTACK
BRYAN GUNN

Goalkeeper Bryan Gunn arrived at Carrow Road in October 1986 following a £100,000 transfer from Aberdeen. Over the next 12 years he amassed 477 appearances for the club and became one of the most popular players to ever pull on the Norwich shirt.

An outstanding shot-stopper, Gunn controlled his area with authority and was also comfortable with the ball at his feet. His performances twice saw him collect the Barry Butler Memorial Trophy as the club's player of the season.

A key player in Mike Walker's 1992-93 side that battled for Premier League title - Gunn played in all six of the club's UEFA Cup fixtures the following season.

CITY APPEARANCES:

APPEARANCES	LEAGUE	FA CUP	LEAGUE CUP	OTHERS*
477	390	2	38	22

SCOTLAND INTERNATIONAL:

APPEARANCES
6

INTERNATIONAL DEBUT:

SCOTLAND 1-3 EGYPT · MAY 16, 1990

JAMAL
LEWIS

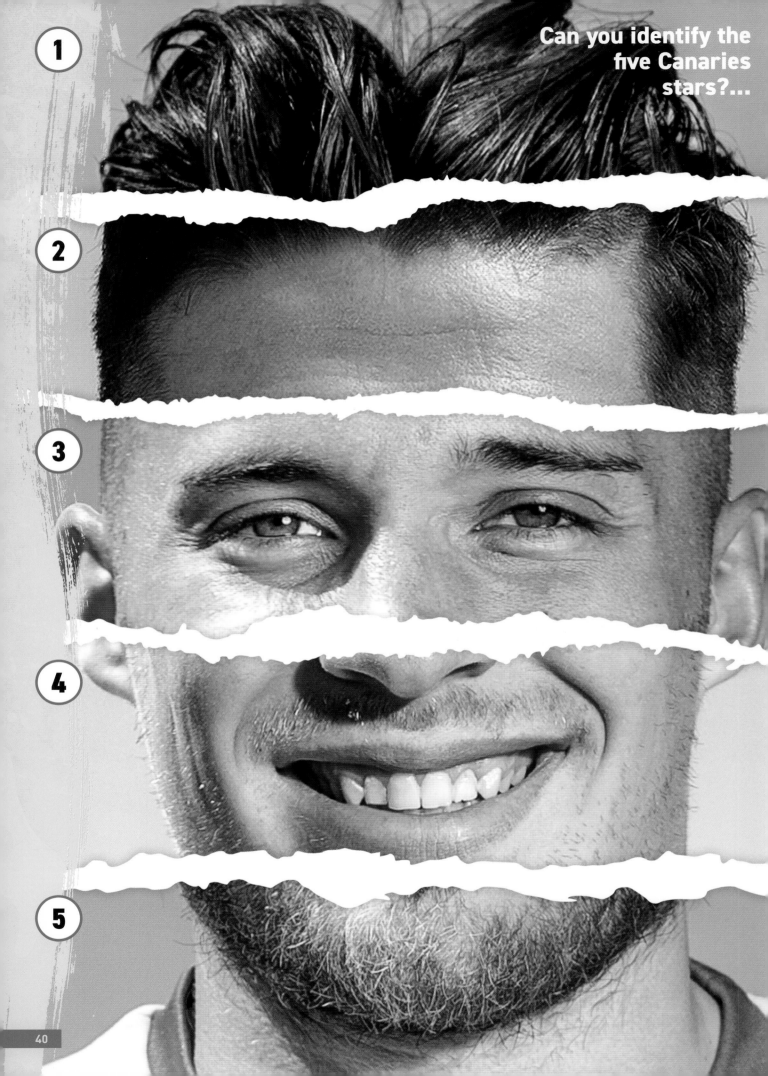

1

2

3

4

5

...and the three here?

6 **7** **8**

WHO ARE YER?

ANSWERS ON PAGE 62

BEN MARSHALL

THE FLIP FLAP
#BOY'SGOTSKILLS

Practise! Practise! Practise!

1. Start by getting familiar with the leg movement.

Push the ball with the outside of your foot.

TIP: Try performing the movement while hopping

TIP: Practise performing the movement while moving forwards and backwards

2. Then move your foot around the ball and bring it back in towards your body.

AKA 'the Elastico'

This move is used by many players and was made famous first by Rivelino in the 1970s and more recently by Ronaldinho. It is a simple technique and done right, really works! The idea behind it is to unbalance your defender by moving the ball one way before using some tricky footwork to move off in another direction!

3. Once you're familiar with the movement, try it while dribbling the ball forward.

TIP: Work on perfecting the technique, then when you're ready you can start moving the ball further away from your body to really confuse your defender

4. Push the ball with the outside of your foot, away from your body. As your defender moves in the direction of the ball...

5. ...Move your foot around the ball, drag it back across your body and move off in the other direction.

We take a look at three great Canaries games from last season...

<<REWIND

IPSWICH 0 NORWICH 1

OCTOBER 22, 2017

It was scrappy, it was nervy, it was tight. But City triumphed once again thanks to a sweet James Maddison strike in the 59th minute.

City rode their luck in the opening skirmishes, with Joe Garner and David McGoldrick missing chances to give Ipswich the lead. But the longer the match went on, the more Norwich - who had gone eight matches unbeaten - started to exert control.

The deadlock was broken when Yanic Wildschut broke forward down the left. Marco Stiepermann took it off him level with the area, and found Maddison just inside the box. With still plenty to do, he composed himself before firing into the bottom corner.

CHELSEA 1 NORWICH 1

JANUARY 17, 2018

City had already had their hearts broken once by a Premier League giant last season, when Arsenal equalised late at the Emirates to take the Carabao Cup tie into extra-time. Now there were heading back to London, this time to Stamford Bridge, and this time in the FA Cup.

Norwich had deservedly held Chelsea to a stalemate at Carrow Road, and more than held their own in London. Michy Batshuayi gave Chelsea a 55th-minute lead, but the Norwich fans went wild in injury time when Jamal Lewis brilliantly nodded home a Timm Klose cross to take the game into extra-time.

An action-packed extra-time saw two Chelsea players sent off late on, but the match was to be settled by penalties. Chelsea scored all of theirs, and Nelson Oliveira was the unlucky Canary to miss. But Norwich headed back to Norfolk after putting on another brave, excellent display against one of the country's best teams.

NORWICH 1 IPSWICH 1

FEBRUARY 18, 2018

For six agonising minutes, it looked like Ipswich were about to triumph in the East Anglian derby for the first time in nine years.

An even game exploded into life in the 89th minute when Luke Chambers headed in from a corner, and celebrated in front of the home fans. Without a win in the derby since 2009, the Ipswich fans were ecstatic.

Norwich didn't give up, though. With the clock ticking over to 95 minutes, Grant Hanley chased what looked like a lost cause on the right in front of the Barclay. He kept the ball in on the byline, looked up and delivered an inch-perfect cross that was met by Timm Klose, who powered in the header to cause absolute pandemonium around Carrow Road.

That dramatic draw made it 10 games unbeaten for City in the derby.

1 Who scored the Canaries' first League goal last season?

ANSWER

ANSWER

What was the score when the Canaries knocked Brentford out of the League Cup?

2

3 Who top scored last season with 14 league goals?

ANSWER

4

City's highest goalscoring performance last season was against which team and what was the score?

ANSWER

5 How many clean sheets did the Canaries keep in the League in 2017-18?

ANSWER

ANSWER

Which player made the most League appearances in 2017-18 with 46?

6

2017-18 END OF TERM EXAM

How much did you learn about the Canaries last campaign?

7

Who was City's first home league win of 2017-18 against?

ANSWER

8

ANSWER

Which Canaries player received the most yellow cards in the League last season?

9

ANSWER

Who scored the goals when Norwich beat Leeds United 2-1 at Carrow Road

10

How many goals did City score in the League last season?

ANSWER

<<REWIND

GRANT HANLEY JOINS THE CELEBRATIONS FOR ALEXANDER TETTEY'S GOAL V PRESTON NORTH END

JOY AS JORDAN RHODES NETS THE FIRST V WBA

ONEL HERNANDEZ CELEBRATES HIS INJURY-TIME EQUALISER AGAINST BIRMINGHAM CITY

TEEMU PUKKI OPENS THE SCORING V PRESTON NORTH END

JORDAN RHODES SALUTES THE CROWD AFTER HIS STRIKE AT SHEFFIELD UNITED

PREDICTION FOR PREMIER LEAGUE WINNERS:

Liverpool

YOUR
PREDICTION:

PREDICTION FOR CHAMPIONSHIP WINNERS:

Norwich City

YOUR
PREDICTION:

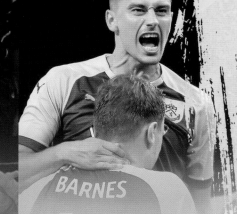

PREDICTION FOR FA CUP WINNERS:

Burnley

YOUR
PREDICTION:

PREDICTION FOR PREMIER LEAGUE RUNNERS-UP:

Manchester City

YOUR
PREDICTION:

PREDICTION FOR CHAMPIONSHIP RUNNERS-UP:

Derby County

YOUR
PREDICTION:

FAST FORWARD>>

Here are our predictions for 2018-19...

What do you think will happen?

2018-19 PREDICTIONS

PREDICTION FOR PREMIER LEAGUE TOP SCORER:

Harry Kane

YOUR
PREDICTION:

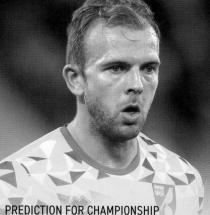

PREDICTION FOR CHAMPIONSHIP TOP SCORER:

Jordan Rhodes

YOUR
PREDICTION:

PREDICTION FOR LEAGUE CUP WINNERS:

Arsenal

YOUR
PREDICTION:

#BOY'S GOT SKILLS
THE OKOCHA STEP-OVER

Jay-Jay Okocha was one of the best tricksters the Premier League has ever seen. He was effortless in getting past his opponents and here we take a look at how to perform one of his most famous moves...

1. While running...

...roll the ball with the inside of your right foot across your body to the left.

2. Fake like you're going to hit it with your left foot...

TIP:
Roll the ball far enough out across your body so it doesn't get stuck under your feet.

Tip:
Practise until you can master the move off both feet!

3. ...but step over it instead!

4. While you're performing the step over...

...do a quick body feint to the right to help throw off your opponent.

5. Continue going left...

...leaving your opponent wondering what just happened!

TEEMU PUKKI

49

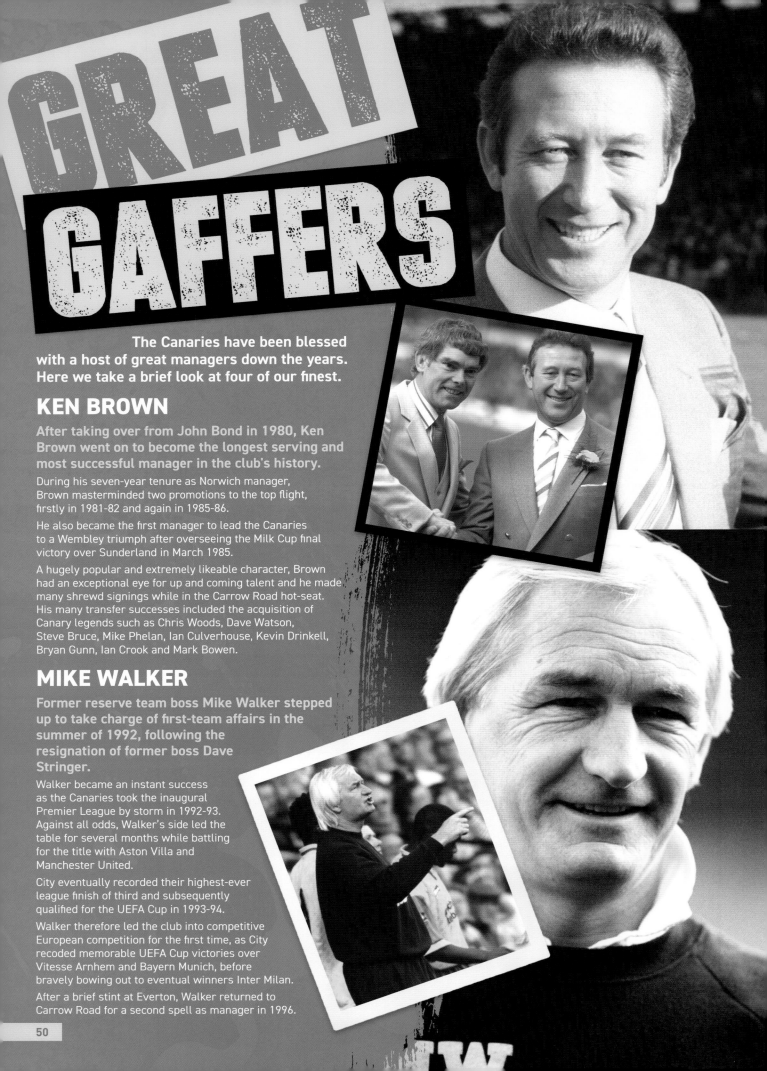

GREAT GAFFERS

The Canaries have been blessed with a host of great managers down the years. Here we take a brief look at four of our finest.

KEN BROWN

After taking over from John Bond in 1980, Ken Brown went on to become the longest serving and most successful manager in the club's history.

During his seven-year tenure as Norwich manager, Brown masterminded two promotions to the top flight, firstly in 1981-82 and again in 1985-86.

He also became the first manager to lead the Canaries to a Wembley triumph after overseeing the Milk Cup final victory over Sunderland in March 1985.

A hugely popular and extremely likeable character, Brown had an exceptional eye for up and coming talent and he made many shrewd signings while in the Carrow Road hot-seat. His many transfer successes included the acquisition of Canary legends such as Chris Woods, Dave Watson, Steve Bruce, Mike Phelan, Ian Culverhouse, Kevin Drinkell, Bryan Gunn, Ian Crook and Mark Bowen.

MIKE WALKER

Former reserve team boss Mike Walker stepped up to take charge of first-team affairs in the summer of 1992, following the resignation of former boss Dave Stringer.

Walker became an instant success as the Canaries took the inaugural Premier League by storm in 1992-93. Against all odds, Walker's side led the table for several months while battling for the title with Aston Villa and Manchester United.

City eventually recorded their highest-ever league finish of third and subsequently qualified for the UEFA Cup in 1993-94.

Walker therefore led the club into competitive European competition for the first time, as City recoded memorable UEFA Cup victories over Vitesse Arnhem and Bayern Munich, before bravely bowing out to eventual winners Inter Milan.

After a brief stint at Everton, Walker returned to Carrow Road for a second spell as manager in 1996.

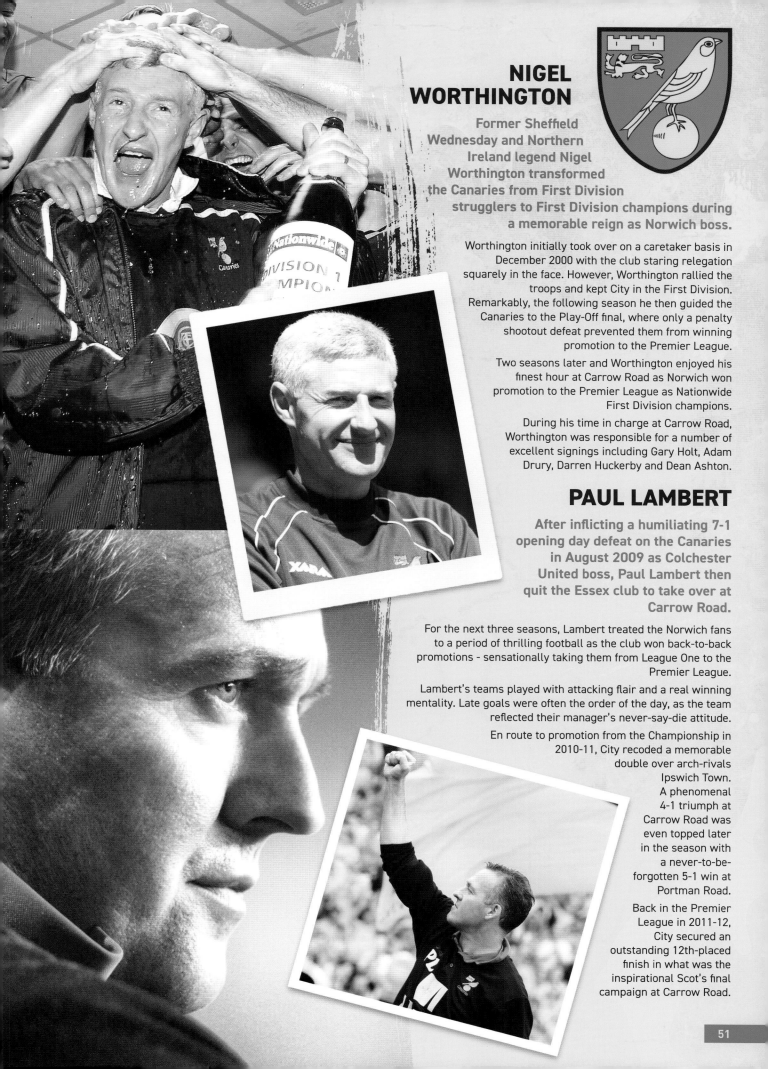

NIGEL WORTHINGTON

Former Sheffield Wednesday and Northern Ireland legend Nigel Worthington transformed the Canaries from First Division strugglers to First Division champions during a memorable reign as Norwich boss.

Worthington initially took over on a caretaker basis in December 2000 with the club staring relegation squarely in the face. However, Worthington rallied the troops and kept City in the First Division. Remarkably, the following season he then guided the Canaries to the Play-Off final, where only a penalty shootout defeat prevented them from winning promotion to the Premier League.

Two seasons later and Worthington enjoyed his finest hour at Carrow Road as Norwich won promotion to the Premier League as Nationwide First Division champions.

During his time in charge at Carrow Road, Worthington was responsible for a number of excellent signings including Gary Holt, Adam Drury, Darren Huckerby and Dean Ashton.

PAUL LAMBERT

After inflicting a humiliating 7-1 opening day defeat on the Canaries in August 2009 as Colchester United boss, Paul Lambert then quit the Essex club to take over at Carrow Road.

For the next three seasons, Lambert treated the Norwich fans to a period of thrilling football as the club won back-to-back promotions - sensationally taking them from League One to the Premier League.

Lambert's teams played with attacking flair and a real winning mentality. Late goals were often the order of the day, as the team reflected their manager's never-say-die attitude.

En route to promotion from the Championship in 2010-11, City recoded a memorable double over arch-rivals Ipswich Town. A phenomenal 4-1 triumph at Carrow Road was even topped later in the season with a never-to-be-forgotten 5-1 win at Portman Road.

Back in the Premier League in 2011-12, City secured an outstanding 12th-placed finish in what was the inspirational Scot's final campaign at Carrow Road.

FIRST ELEVEN

Choose your all-time First Eleven, put their names and numbers on the back of the shirts, then colour them in!

SPOT THE BALL

The ball is missing from this photo, where should it be?

WHAT BALL?

Can you figure out which is the real ball in this photo?

ONEL HERNÁNDEZ

Magic MOMENT 15'

PLAY OFF *Success*

FIXTURE: Sky Bet Championship Play-Off final

DATE: Monday, May 25, 2015

SCORE: Norwich City 2 Middlesbrough 0

VENUE: Wembley Stadium

ATTENDANCE: 85,656

13 KONSTANTOPOULOS

18 WHITEHEAD

4 JOHNSON

AYALA 4

GIBSON 6

22 REDMOND

10 JEROME

7 LEADBITTER

8 CLAYTON

22 REDMOND

3 FRIEND

2 WHITTAKER

TOMLIN 10

HOOLAHAN 14

The Yellow Army were already in seventh heaven after Cameron Jerome's 12th minute goal had given City the lead in the 2014-15 Sky Bet Championship final at Wembley.

Just three minutes later and things got even better for the yellow and green masses, as City doubled their lead and took a giant step towards Premier League promotion.

Left-back Martin Olsson began the slickest of moves by winning possession down the left and 17 passes later Nathan Redmond latched on to Steven Whittaker's beautifully weighted ball down the right channel and drilled home the Canaries' all-important second goal.

Here is a list of 20 Canaries heroes. All but one of their surnames are hidden in the grid, can you work out who is missing?

I ♥ NCFC

```
A Q A D D F I H S A C S F J B A P L X N K M
W G F U A S V Q E D D C F G E C U R B K L Z
O E N P S G P W Z E V V K N N R S H J C X J
Y A H K E N X B W T E R O X L A F P B A S H
I J F B C T M J T Y F T R Y J A E K G M D C
K R D G N H E Y G O T Z L C H L G D N F Q V
J F L V M K S R W U I G U I D S T R E B O R
L O D B E W M U S U N V T M Q P W R H P B E
L R I V R O G K U F I N N O I B K S X D E Y
C B S T P Q P O I G J O H U T O Y O J M S O
L E X F P T H U C K E R B Y I Y S T U Y N B
Z S O T R O S Y R T Y U B R C I W D P F Z L
W T R J L Z E Y U I E V Q U P A T O O M C K
Z M E T P D O A W I T U M R R A F K L O V Z
W Y L C H B K F Y J O H R D E E H A N G W H
X D X K E A V B H G I B S L K X B E U F D L
U Y U P C I I M J U H D U E K H I T A W D S
O F G H K W D N N V K J O T N L Q R N E L J
D W E D N I J A S E M T J H L R S V D J P I
T A Q R H A L M E V D L E X K E F B M I Y O
R S V U I Q E H P C T R F Y U A R C G C I W
A L G I F O Y S R B F K C G J T H O S G A D
E V S B E L L A M Y W S Z F L Y N V M U P P
A R J S B S X N V N D L N B A V B H J K Q L
T G E G W K C L Z M V M K H F U N A H S A F
```

Ron **Ashman**	Ron **Davies**	Duncan **Forbes**	Martin **O'Neill**
Craig **Bellamy**	John **Deehan**	Jeremy **Goss**	Martin **Peters**
Phil **Boyer**	Adam **Drury**	Bryan **Gunn**	Iwan **Roberts**
Steve **Bruce**	Darren **Eadie**	Grant **Holt**	Chris **Sutton**
Barry **Butler**	Justin **Fashanu**	Darren **Huckerby**	Chris **Woods**

ANSWERS ON PAGE 62

Shirt 1
RLVOELPOI
1

Shirt 2
ALUMHF
2

Shirt 3
FEEHFLDIS NIEUDT
3

Shirt 4
RNGBIHMMIA TIYC
4

Shirt 5
TEWS AMH DUTNIE
5

Shirt 6
YCTSLRA LAPEAC
6

SHIRT SHUFFLE

Here are the away shirts of
12 Premier League and Championship
clubs, but their team names have been jumbled up!

Can you figure out who's who?

Shirt 7
OONEUMTBRUH
7

Shirt 8
NQESEU RKAP GRARNES
8

Shirt 9
KOETS TCIY
9

Shirt 10
WESATNELC TUNEDI
10

Shirt 11
ROTPENS HRTNO NDE
11

Shirt 12
NATOS LAVIL
12

ADAM JAMES DRURY
AUGUST 29, 1978
COTTENHAM, CAMBRIDGESHIRE

POSITION:

LEFT-BACK

CANARIES DEBUT:

NORWICH CITY 2-1 GRIMSBY TOWN
NATIONWIDE DIVISION ONE
MARCH 31, 2001

CITY PLAYER OF THE SEASON:

2002-03

STAT ATTACK
ADAM DRURY

Captain of the Canaries'
2003-04 Nationwide First Division
title-winning side, long-serving left-back Adam Drury joined
Norwich City in March 2001 from Peterborough United.

Signed by Nigel Worthington, Drury went on to enjoy 11 seasons
at Carrow Road while amassing over 350 games for the club.
He was an extremely reliable and consistent defender who excelled
in one-on-one situations. His polished performances in 2002-03
saw him voted Player of the Season.

Drury's time at Carrow Road was certainly eventful as he experienced
three promotions, two relegations and a Play-Off final. His loyalty to
the Canary cause was rewarded with a testimonial match against
Scottish giants Celtic in May 2012.

CITY APPEARANCES:

APPEARANCES	LEAGUE	FA CUP	LEAGUE CUP	PLAY-OFFS
361	326	18	13	4

CITY GOALS:

GOALS	LEAGUE
4	4

IVO PINTO

How's your knowledge of the laws of the game?
You think you can do better than the man in the middle?
here's you chance to prove it...

HEY REF!

1. Ben Marshall shoots for goal from 25 yards. His fierce drive deflects off your head, wrong-footing the keeper, on its way into the back of the net. What's your call?

A: You award an indirect free-kick to the opposition.
B: It's a goal!
C: You give a drop-ball from where you were hit by the ball.

2. Jordan Rhodes strikes for goal from six yards, but as he shoots, the ball bursts and stops just before the goal line. Alert, he follows up and taps the ball home. What's your call?

A: It's a goal!
B: You award a penalty kick to the Canaries.
C: No goal and you restart with a drop ball where the ball burst.

3. Matt Jarvis sends the keeper the wrong way from the penalty spot, but his effort hits the post and rebounds straight to Tom Trybull who rifles the ball into the net to score. What is your decision?

A: It's a goal!
B: The spot kick has to be retaken.
C: I award an indirect free-kick to the opposition.

MARSHALL

JARVIS   TRYBULL

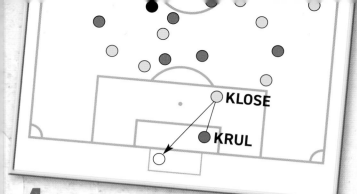

KLOSE

KRUL

4. Tim Krul attempts to take a quick goal kick, but to his horror, it hits Timm Klose who is still in the penalty area and the ball deflects into his own net. What's your call, ref?

A: It's a goal!
B: A corner kick to the opposing team
C: The Goal kick has to be retaken.

5. Standing in his own penalty area, Tim Krul catches the ball directly from teammate Grant Hanley's throw-in. What is your decision?

A: Everything's fine. Play on.
B: You award the opposing team an indirect free-kick.
C: A yellow card for Krul and a penalty for the opposing team.

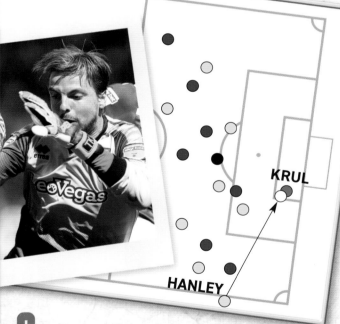

KRUL

HANLEY

6. You have decided Dennis Srbeny's spot kick must be re-taken after an infringement by the keeper. This time Jordan Rhodes steps forward to take the kick. Is that allowed?

A: No, I award an indirect free kick to the opposition.
B: Yes, any City player can re-take the penalty.
C: No, the player who took the initial spot kick, Dennis Srbeny, must retake the kick.

7. You have awarded a drop ball. As you drop the ball, Emiliano Buendía and the opposing player both kick the ball at exactly the same time before it hits the turf. What's your ruling?

A: You show a yellow card to both players for ungentlemanly conduct.
B: You drop the ball again.
C: Play on.

HERNANDEZ

8. Onel Hernandez is on the scoresheet again, tapping in from only three yards out. When he scores, he is slightly ahead of the last defender, but in line with the goalkeeper. What is your decision?

A: Goal. In line with the keeper is not offside.
B: Goal disallowed. Hernandez is offside. To be onside, he must be in line with the second last opponent or the ball.
C: Goal. A player can't be offside inside the six-yard box.

9. Grant Hanley takes a long throw in aiming for the head of Mario Vrančić. No-one makes contact with the ball and it bounces into the net direct from Hanley's throw. What's your call, ref?

A: Goal. Providing there was an attempt to play the ball.
B: Goal. As long as the throw-in was taken correctly.
C: No Goal. A goal can never be scored direct from a throw in.

ANSWERS

PAGE 26 · FAN'TASTIC

Raheem Sterling, Ben Alnwick, Harry Maguire, Jordan Henderson and Harry Kane.

PAGE 34 · GUESS THE CLUB

1. Ajax. 2. Paris Saint-Germain. 3. Bayern Munich.
4. Sporting Lisbon. 5. Real Madrid. 6. Arsenal. 7. Celtic.
8. Juventus. 9. Barcelona. 10. Club Brugge.

PAGE 40 · WHO ARE YER?

1. Ben Marshall. 2. Emiliano Buendía. 3. Moritz Leitner.
4. Felix Passlack. 5. Teemu Pukki. 6. Christoph Zimmermann.
7. Todd Cantwell. 8. Grant Hanley.

PAGE 44 · 2018/19 END OF TERM EXAM

1. Nélson Oliveira. 2. 3-1. 3. James Maddison. 4. Charlton Athletic,
4-1. 5. 15. 6. Angus Gunn. 7. QPR. 8. Alexander Tettey, 9.
9. Wes Hoolahan and Josh Murphy. 10. 49.

PAGE 53 · SPOT THE BALL

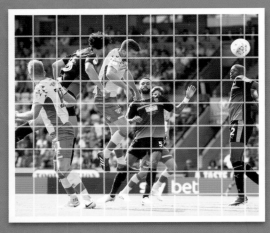

PAGE 53 · WHICH BALL?

Ball C.

PAGE 56 · HERO HUNT

Jeremy Goss.

PAGE 57 · SHIRT SHUFFLE

1. Liverpool. 2. Fulham. 3. Sheffield United. 4. Birmingham City.
5. West Ham United. 6. Crystal Palace. 7. Bournemouth.
8. Queens Park Rangers. 9. Stoke City. 10. Newcastle United.
11. Preston North End. 12. Aston Villa

PAGE 60 · ASK THE REF

1. B. 2. C. 3. A. 4. C. 5. B. 6. B. 7. B. 8. B. 9. C.